INTRODUCTION

AN ENCYCLICAL IS A LETTER TO THE WORLD FROM THE POPE, one that lays out his views on Church teaching or other matters. Here Pope Francis, working with a letter begun by Pope Benedict XVI, has chosen to reflect on faith and what it means for our world, our Church communities, and our personal growth. The Latin name for this encyclical is *Lumen Fidei* (Light of Faith).

The pope believes that our world is hungering for the light revealed by God, the light that illumines our entire life journey. This light, he says, comes from the risen Christ, the "morning star that never sets." He says that faith is not a light that scatters all our darkness, but a "lamp that guides us in the night and suffices for the journey."

We invite you to walk with Pope Francis for thirty days, reflecting on some of his teachings about faith. On each of these pages, we offer a brief thought from the encyclical, a related Scripture passage, a prayer, and a practice in response to the pope's message.

May this booklet inspire your own growth in faith and put you in closer touch with Jesus, the "burning flame" who brightens and sustains our lives.

CONTENTS

1. Open my eyes 3
2. Faith is my light...... 4
3. Advancing toward God.................5
4. Saying amen............... 6
5. A dazzling light 7
6. Through Jesus' eyes 8
7. A deeper level 9
8. God's gift to us...... 10
9. What faith teaches 11
10. God's immense love 12
11. Into the depths 13
12. Truth embraces me.14
13. Jesus lights the way 15
14. All in the circle 16
15. Called to explore .. 17
16. Sharing the gift.....18
17. A rich seed...............19
18. Faith passed on.......20
19. Sharing memories...21
20. For every generation................22
21. Faith and baptism ...23
22. Precious nourishment 24
23. Sacraments and memory...............25
24. Fullness of life...... 26
25. Four ways to faith..27
26. A great joy 28
27. On the same rock .. 29
28. A vocation to love...................... 30
29. Suffering and faith 31
30. Mary our model......32

The Scripture quotes were chosen by Gwen Costello, who also wrote the prayers and practices. Cover photo: Jeffrey Bruno/Catholic News Agency
Copyright © 2013 Twenty-Third Publications, a division of Bayard;
One Montauk Avenue, New London, CT 06320. 860-437-3012 or 800-3210-411, www.23rdpublications.com. No part of this publication may be reproduced in any manner without prior written permission of the publisher. All rights reserved.
ISBN 978-1-62785-002-5 ■ Printed in the U.S.A.

5th Printing 2013

1 | OPEN MY EYES

Faith helps us to "see" at a deeper level because we have a light that illumines our entire lives. This light is the risen Christ, who is with us like a morning star that never sets.

SCRIPTURE
I am the light of the world. Whoever follows me... will have the light of life. *John 8:12*

PRAYER
Walk with me, Jesus, as I ponder the meaning of my faith. Open my mind and heart to the pope's words, that I might not only understand them, but also let them touch my life at the deepest level. Help me to truly "see" the beauty and importance of my faith and to stay close to you in all I do. Amen.

PRACTICE
Today I will spend time thinking about how I can practice my faith at a deeper level, guided by Jesus, my light.

2 | FAITH IS MY LIGHT

If the flame of faith dies out, all other lights begin to fade. The light our faith gives us can light up every aspect of our human existence.

SCRIPTURE
Jesus prayed: "I thank you Father, Lord of heaven and earth, because you have hidden these things from the wise and intelligent and have revealed them to your little ones." *Matthew 11:25*

PRAYER
How fortunate I am, loving God, that you are speaking to me through the words of Jesus and Pope Francis about my faith! May my faith in you grow stronger, and may I become one of your "little ones" who grasps how important it is in my daily life. May the flame of my faith grow until it becomes a great and beautiful fire of love! Amen.

PRACTICE
Today I will light a candle and sit quietly for a few moments recalling that faith is my guiding light.

3 | ADVANCING TOWARD GOD

The three virtues of faith, hope, and charity are the driving force of our Christian lives as we advance toward our loving God.

SCRIPTURE
Keep alert, stand firm in your faith, be courageous, be strong. Let all that you do be done in love. *1 Corinthians 16:13–14*

PRAYER
Fill my heart and soul with your gifts of faith, hope, and charity, loving God. May these spiritual gifts sustain and nourish me as I journey through life. Help me to keep alert and strong, so that all I do might be done in love, with deep faith, and with abiding hope. Amen.

PRACTICE
Inspired by my faith in God, I will offer love and encouragement to a family member or co-worker today.

4 | SAYING AMEN

All the threads and promises of the Old Testament point toward Christ, who is our great teacher and guide. Christ helps us say "yes" to all that God asks of us.

SCRIPTURE

All the promises of God find their Yes in Christ. That is why it is through him that we utter our "Amen" to God when we worship together. *2 Corinthians 1:20*

PRAYER

Jesus, beloved Savior, help me to understand that when I say "amen" to you when I receive the Eucharist, I am saying "yes" to all that you did and taught. Through you, I can say yes to God in all my daily activities—at home, at work, in my parish, and in my neighborhood. Strengthen me to say this "yes" with all my heart, mind, and soul. Amen.

PRACTICE

As I do my daily chores and activities today, I will say "yes" to acknowledge that God is with me, guiding, healing, and loving me.

5 | A DAZZLING LIGHT

When we contemplate Jesus' death, our faith grows stronger, and, like a "dazzling light," it helps us experience Christ's deep and enduring love for us, a love that embraced death to bring us salvation.

SCRIPTURE

For God who said, "Let light shine out of darkness," has shone in our hearts so we in turn can make known the glory of God shining on the face of Jesus Christ. *2 Corinthians 4:6*

PRAYER

Loving God, thank you for the great gift of your Son, Jesus Christ. May I, through my acts of love and service this day, let his "dazzling light" shine out to everyone I meet. Forgive me for those times I fail to be the light of Christ for others, and help my faith, hope, and love grow stronger. Amen.

PRACTICE

Today I will say this little prayer often: Jesus, my light, shine through me.

6 | THROUGH JESUS' EYES

Having faith is more than just gazing at Jesus. It helps us see things as Jesus himself sees them, with his own eyes. With faith we can share in Jesus' way of seeing.

SCRIPTURE
Now faith is the assurance of things hoped for, the conviction of things not seen. *Hebrews 11:1*

PRAYER
What a great gift faith is, dear God! Help me to take to heart the words of Pope Francis that when I have faith I can see things as Jesus sees them. Also, give me hope to believe that, even when I forget to look at life through the eyes of Jesus, you are still always with me, loving and forgiving me. Amen.

PRACTICE
I will try today, through the gift of faith, to see life in fresh, new ways.

7 | A DEEPER LEVEL

Our faith in the Son of God made man in Jesus of Nazareth helps us to understand reality at the deepest level and to see how much God loves us and guides us toward himself.

SCRIPTURE

Jesus said, "I tell you the truth, if you have faith… you can say to this mountain, 'Go, throw yourself into the sea,' and it will be done." *Matthew 21:21*

PRAYER

Increase my faith, O God, that I might listen more closely to your beloved Son, Jesus. The Holy Father assures me that Jesus will open my eyes to your presence in my life as I move daily toward you. Give me the precious gift of "seeing," and may Jesus be my guide. Amen.

PRACTICE

I will spend ten minutes in silence today, listening for God and being open to whatever God is asking me to do.

8 | GOD'S GIFT TO US

Even when people obey the commandments and do good works, they can still be self-centered, especially if they fail to see that all goodness comes from God.

SCRIPTURE
It is because of Christ that salvation is ours through faith. This is not our own doing; it is God's gift. *Ephesians 2:8*

PRAYER
I know that I am often self-centered, O God, especially when I do good deeds and expect something in return. Even when I pray, I sometimes think of myself as good and holy. But all goodness comes from you. Help me to believe this and to open my heart to you more fully. I ask this through Jesus Christ my Lord. Amen.

PRACTICE
I will try to reflect God's goodness in all that I do today and with everyone I meet.

9 | WHAT FAITH TEACHES

Faith reveals that Christ has been given to us as a great gift and that he changes us completely, dwells within us, and bestows on us the light to understand life, both our origin and the end of life.

SCRIPTURE
Your faith—of greater worth than gold, which perishes even though refined by fire—may be proved genuine and may result in praise, glory, and honor when Jesus Christ is revealed. *1 Peter 1:7*

PRAYER
Dear God, may I be open to your gift of faith offered through your Son, Jesus. I want to be changed, open to his presence, and receptive to all that he teaches. I want to treasure my faith and understand what a valuable gift it is. Help me in all this, and give me the light that leads to understanding. Amen.

PRACTICE
I will thank God throughout my day for giving me the valuable and treasured gift of faith.

10 | GOD'S IMMENSE LOVE

*We begin to understand what faith means
when we open ourselves to the immense love of God
that changes us inwardly and enables us to see
our lives with new eyes.*

SCRIPTURE

For it is by grace you have been saved, through faith—and this not from yourselves; it is the gift of God. *Ephesians 2:8*

PRAYER

Great and loving God, I would like with all my heart to experience your immense love and to be changed—made new—so that I can see your hand in all things. Thank you for the gift of faith. Through it, may I see my life with new eyes. Amen.

PRACTICE

I will try to experience everything I do today with new eyes, with wonder.

11 | INTO THE DEPTHS

With their own eyes the apostles saw the risen Jesus and they believed; they were able to peer into the depths of what they were seeing and to confess their faith in the Son of God.

SCRIPTURE

Let us draw near to God with a sincere heart in full assurance of faith, having our hearts sprinkled to cleanse us from a guilty conscience and having our bodies washed with pure water. *Hebrews 10:22*

PRAYER

I've often thought, dear God, that if I could see Jesus as the apostles saw him, I would be a whole new person. And yet I do believe that you are calling me too to look at Jesus and believe in his teachings about your kingdom. Sprinkle my heart and cleanse me from anything that keeps me from loving and serving you. Amen.

PRACTICE

In my heart, I will "confess my faith in the Son of God" at least three times today.

12 | TRUTH EMBRACES ME

Believers should not be presumptuous; rather, truth leads to humility. We know it is not ourselves possessing truth; it is truth that embraces and possesses us.

SCRIPTURE

Jesus said to them, "I tell you the truth: those who have faith in me will do what I have been doing. They will do even greater things than these, because I am going to the Father." *John 14:12*

PRAYER

Loving God, I want your truth, as revealed by Jesus, to embrace and possess me in all that I do in my life's journey. Pope Francis assures me that all good things come from you. You are as close to me as my own heartbeat when I strive to place my trust in you and believe. May I believe and live this with all my heart. Amen.

PRACTICE

I will pray to the Holy Spirit often today to give me deeper and more genuine faith.

13 | JESUS LIGHTS THE WAY

The light of faith in Jesus illumines the path of all those who seek God, and makes a distinctly Christian contribution to dialogue with the followers of other religions.

SCRIPTURE

Let us run with perseverance the race that is set before us, looking to Jesus the pioneer and perfecter of our faith, who for the sake of the joy that was set before him endured the cross. *Hebrews 12:1~2*

PRAYER

Thank you, Creator God, for giving me Jesus to light the way. I ask you for courage and perseverance that I might run the race set before me, taking the good with the bad, and enduring my crosses with courage. Help me too to open my heart to those of all other faiths and to respect them and their beliefs. Amen.

PRACTICE

I will try to learn something new today about people with a different religious faith.

14 | ALL IN THE CIRCLE

When we immerse ourselves in the circle of Christ's light, we are capable of understanding and accompanying the path of every man and woman toward God.

SCRIPTURE

Faith comes from hearing the message, and the message is heard through the word of Christ. *Romans 10:17*

PRAYER

As a Christian believer, O God, I see the world through the story of Jesus and his death and resurrection. I want to open my heart to all those of other faiths who are on the path to you in the same spirit in which Jesus welcomed all who approached him. Help me to immerse myself fully in the circle of Christ's light that I might truly "see." Amen.

PRACTICE

I will remember today that all people are God's children, and I will respect each person I meet as such.

15 | CALLED TO EXPLORE

Faith is a light and it draws us into itself, inviting us to explore ever more fully the horizon that it illuminates. Faith invites us to better know the object of our love.

SCRIPTURE

Open yourself to God's Spirit...Hold on to what is good and don't have anything to do with evil.
1 Thessalonians 5:19~22

PRAYER

Come, Father, Son, and Holy Spirit, and give me the light of faith, that I might come to know and love you, the true object of my love and my life. I do want to explore the "horizon" more fully and to be ever open to new discoveries and directions. Help me to hold on to what is good and to share that goodness freely with those I meet. Amen.

PRACTICE

I will imagine myself bathed in the light of faith today, and act accordingly.

16 | SHARING THE GIFT

Those who have opened their hearts to God's love, heard his voice, and received his light, cannot keep this gift to themselves.

SCRIPTURE

God has said, "Let the light shine out of darkness," and this same God shines in our hearts to help us see the glory of God in the face of Jesus.
2 Corinthians 4:6

PRAYER

Pope Francis encourages me, holy God, to open my heart more fully to your love, to hear your voice, and to receive your light. And then he says that the gift of believing has to be shared; I shouldn't keep it to myself. I need your grace that I might learn to share my faith joyfully. Help me to take a first step today. Amen.

PRACTICE

I will try to let the light of my faith "shine out of the darkness" today at home, at work, and in my community.

17 | A RICH SEED

Followers of Christ, in a spirit of poverty, plant a seed so rich that it becomes a great tree, filling the whole world with its fruit.

SCRIPTURE
If you have faith as small as a mustard seed, you can say to this mountain, "Move from here to there," and it will move. Nothing will be impossible for you. *Matthew 17:20*

PRAYER
Jesus my Savior, help me to have the kind of faith you describe, which though as small as a mustard seed, can still do great things for God. I would love to plant the "rich seed" Pope Francis describes and be part of the great movement of faith that fills the whole world. Thank you for walking with me always. Amen.

PRACTICE
Today, I will try to plant a rich seed of faith in someone else's heart.

18 | FAITH PASSED ON

We experience faith and encounter God in our own particular time in history, and faith lights up our journey through time. Faith must be passed on in every age.

SCRIPTURE

If anyone is in Christ, there is a new creation: everything old has passed away. See, everything has become new! All this is from God, who reconciled us to himself through Christ. *2 Corinthians 5:17-18*

PRAYER

I do believe, loving God, that I can experience you here and now, in this very moment of history, and Pope Francis encourages me to "pass on" this belief to everyone I encounter in my daily life so that it might thrive in "every age." Thank you for giving us Jesus, through whom everything becomes new. It gives me great joy to know that you, great God, walk with me this day and always. Amen.

PRACTICE

Each time I pray to God today, I will recall that faith grows when faith is shared.

19 | SHARING MEMORIES

*The Church, just like every family,
has a whole store of memories,
and she passes these on to her children.*

SCRIPTURE
The Spirit and the bride say, "Come." And let everyone who hears say "Come," and let everyone who is thirsty come. Let anyone who desires it take the water of life as a gift. *Revelation 22:17*

PRAYER
I have received the gift of Jesus and his teachings through your Church, O God, and throughout my life I want to pass on my faith by living it. Jesus' gospel words belong in my own "store of memories," as well as the teachings of the Church. You say "Come" and drink of the "water of life," and I want to do this today and always. Amen.

PRACTICE
I will recall the words of the Creed today and how they have guided and shaped me.

20 | FOR EVERY GENERATION

Through doctrine, life, and worship, the Church communicates and passes on all that she herself is, all that she believes, to every generation.

SCRIPTURE

You are no longer strangers and aliens, but you are citizens with the saints and also members of the household of God, built upon the foundation of the apostles and prophets, with Jesus Christ himself as the cornerstone. *Ephesians 2:19~20*

PRAYER

Loving God, I am so happy to be among those who share the doctrine, life, and worship of the Church, a sharing that makes me a "citizen with the saints." May my belief in the doctrines, my living of the faith, and my worship with my parish community contribute to the "passing on" of all the Church is and believes. Thank you for this great privilege. Amen.

PRACTICE

I will be conscious today that I am a member of "God's household."

21 | FAITH AND BAPTISM

In baptism we receive not only a creed to profess but also a particular way of life—one that calls for full engagement and sets us on the path to goodness.

SCRIPTURE

Go therefore and make disciples of all nations, baptizing them in the name of the Father, and of the Son, and of the Holy Spirit, and teaching them everything I have commanded you. And remember I am with you always, to the end of the age. *Matthew 28:19-20*

PRAYER

Dear God, I very much want to be on the path to goodness, and Pope Francis says I am on this path when I live and profess the beliefs of my baptism. Keep me on this path that I might embrace my Christian way of life and willingly share it with others. Thank you for your Son, Jesus Christ, in whose name I have been baptized. Amen.

PRACTICE

I will say throughout the day today: I believe in God, the Father almighty, Creator of heaven and earth.

22 | PRECIOUS NOURISHMENT

The Eucharist, an intimate meeting with Christ, who is truly present, is a priceless gift that nourishes our faith. It is Christ's offering of supreme love, the life-giving gift of himself.

SCRIPTURE

Then he took a loaf of bread, and when he had given thanks, he gave it to them saying, "This is my body which is given for you. Do this in remembrance of me." *Luke 22:19*

PRAYER

Loving God, I believe that the Eucharist is the mystery at the heart of my faith. Jesus gives himself with complete and total love so I can share in your kingdom. Each Sunday I receive the supreme gift of love he offers, "the life-giving gift of himself." Give me courage to go out and live my "amen" in "remembrance of him."

PRACTICE

I will say throughout the day today: I believe in Jesus Christ, his Son, our Lord.

23 | SACRAMENTS AND MEMORY

*When the Church celebrates the sacraments,
she makes a profession of faith in Jesus Christ,
and in this way she keeps her memory of him alive.*

SCRIPTURE
Jesus said…"All things can be done for the one who believes." Immediately the father cried out, "Lord I do believe! Help my unbelief!" *Mark 9:23~24*

PRAYER
Thank you for the sacraments, holy God, for they keep me in touch with you. Each one in its own way is celebrated in memory of Jesus, and in that way our faith is passed on to one another and to those who come after us. Help me to profess my faith in Jesus often, and forgive me when I fail to do so. "Lord, I do believe! Help my unbelief!" Amen.

PRACTICE
Today I will recall that Jesus walks with me always, and when I share this belief with others I am keeping the memory of him alive.

24 | FULLNESS OF LIFE

Through our faith, we profess our love for God, who is the origin and sustainer of all things. With faith, we allow ourselves to be guided by God's love and thus journey to fullness of life.

SCRIPTURE

God is love and those who abide in love abide in God, and God abides in them. *1 John 4:16*

PRAYER

I do love you, O God, and I want to remain in that love, to "abide" in it. Pope Francis says that I do this when I hold fast to my faith. If I do this, I will be guided by you toward fullness of life. Please deepen my faith each day of my life journey, and help me to share my faith with others along the way. Amen.

PRACTICE

Today I will be especially generous in my love toward my family members, friends, co-workers, and those in need.

25 | FOUR WAYS TO FAITH

The Church hands down four ingredients that make up the storehouse of her memory: the profession of faith, the celebration of the sacraments, observing the Ten Commandments, and prayer.

SCRIPTURE
I declare that your steadfast love is established forever. *Psalm 89:2*

PRAYER
Help me to take heart, dear God, from the words of Pope Francis: that by professing my faith, by celebrating Christ's presence in the sacraments, by living your Ten Commandments, and by praying daily, I am sharing in the Church's memories. In all these ways, may I be conscious of the great gift you are, O Holy One. Through my faith, "I will sing of your steadfast love." Amen.

ACTION
I will take time today to reflect on the four elements of faith described by Pope Francis.

26 | A GREAT JOY

One of the great joys of faith is a unity of vision in one body and one spirit. St. Leo the Great once said: "If faith is not one, then it is not faith."

SCRIPTURE

So, in Christ we, though many, form one body, and each member belongs to all the others. *Romans 12:5*

PRAYER

Loving God, when I am at Mass, I do feel the great "joy of faith" when all those around me proclaim the same beliefs. We are there together, united in our faith in Jesus Christ your Son. I want to keep this joy alive in my daily life and proclaim my faith often throughout my day. Keep me firm in this resolve. Amen.

PRACTICE

I will say throughout the day today: I believe in the holy, catholic Church and the communion of saints.

27 | ON THE SAME ROCK

When we profess the same faith, we are standing firm on the same rock, we are made new by the same Spirit of love, and we shine out as one light.

SCRIPTURE
See, the home of God is among mortals. He will dwell with them as their God; they will be his people, and God himself will be with them.
Revelation 21:3

PRAYER
The words of Pope Francis make me happy, O God, for through them I feel connected to all who express their faith in you. I want to be standing on the "same rock" and to be "made new" by the Spirit of love. I want to "shine out as one light." Thank you for these gifts of faith and the joy they bring. Amen.

PRACTICE
I will try to remember today that I am "made new by the Spirit of love."

28 | A VOCATION TO LOVE

Faith is not a refuge for the fainthearted, but rather it enhances our lives and makes us aware of our magnificent calling, our vocation to love.

SCRIPTURE
Beloved, since God loved us so much, we also ought to love one another. *1 John 4:11*

PRAYER
O loving God, it's not easy to love others, especially when this involves reaching out beyond my own family and friends. Certainly faith and its accompanying "vocation to love" are not for the fainthearted. Yet faith and love are part of what Pope Francis says is a "magnificent calling," and with your help I want to be worthy of this calling. Amen.

PRACTICE
I will consciously practice at least one act of generous self-giving today and thus respond to my vocation to love.

29 | SUFFERING AND FAITH

Suffering in this life is inevitable, yet it can have meaning when we place our love and trust in our God, who never abandons us. Our suffering can thus lead to growth in faith and love.

SCRIPTURE

They will no longer be hungry or thirsty; the sun will not strike them, nor any scorching heat, for the Lamb…will be their shepherd, and he will guide them to springs of the water of life. *Revelation 7:16~17*

PRAYER

I know, O God, that my everyday sufferings are nothing compared to what so many people have to endure. I pray for them, and I ask you to help me see my own suffering as a path to "growth in faith and love." May Jesus my good shepherd guide me—and all those who suffer—toward the "water of life," where suffering is no more. Amen.

PRACTICE

I will place my suffering in God's hands today and trust that God is with me.

30 | MARY OUR MODEL

The Mother of the Lord is the perfect icon of faith. Her cousin Saint Elizabeth said about her, "Blessed is she who believed!"

SCRIPTURE
And Mary said, "My soul magnifies the Lord, and my spirit rejoices in God my Savior." *Luke 1:46–47*

PRAYER
Hail Mary, full of grace, blessed are you among women. You believed in God's word even in the face of great difficulty. You endured deep suffering as you saw your beloved Son suffer and die. And yet you believed. Pray for me, Mary, that I might have a deep and enduring faith in God's promises to me, and that I might follow your Son, Jesus, as faithfully as you did. Amen.

PRACTICE
I will say this prayer throughout the day: Holy Mary, Mother of God, pray for me.